FIVE 5 FINGER PIANO

The Very Best Of BROADWAY

T0052900

ISBN 0-634-06636-6

HAL•LEONARD®
CORPORATION
7777 W. BLUEMOUND RD. P.O. BOX 13819 MILWAUKEE, WI 53213

Visit Hal Leonard Online at
www.halleonard.com

The Very Best Of BROADWAY

Hello, Dolly!

from HELLO, DOLLY!

Music and Lyric by
Jerry Herman

Moderately

Hel - lo, Dol - ly, well, hel - lo, Dol - ly, it's so

Duet Part (Student plays one octave higher than written.)

Moderately

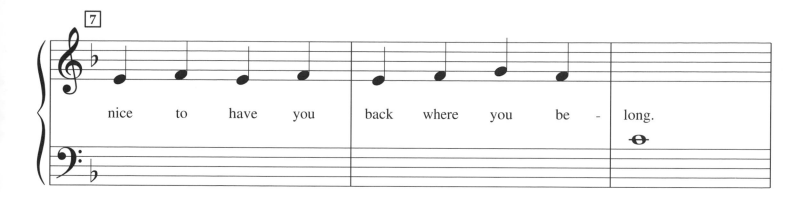

nice to have you back where you be - long.

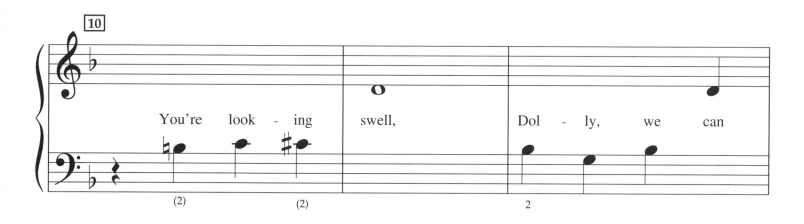

You're look - ing swell, Dol - ly, we can

(2) (2) 2

tell, Dol - ly, you're still glow - in', you're still

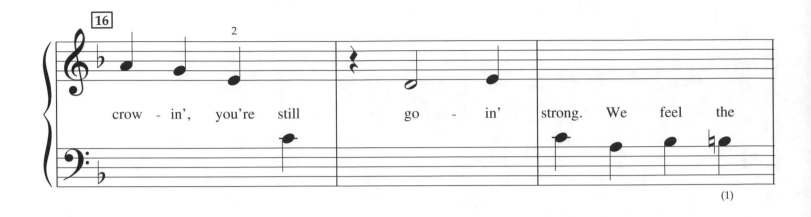

crow - in', you're still go - in' strong. We feel the

(1)

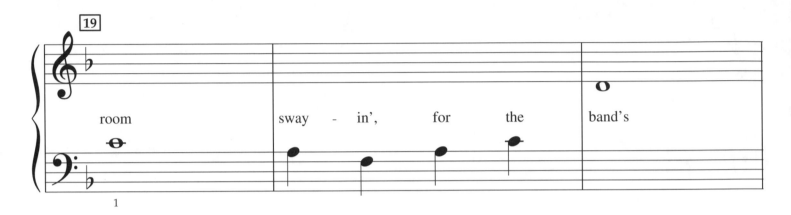

room sway - in', for the band's

1

play - in' one of your old fav - 'rite songs from 'way back

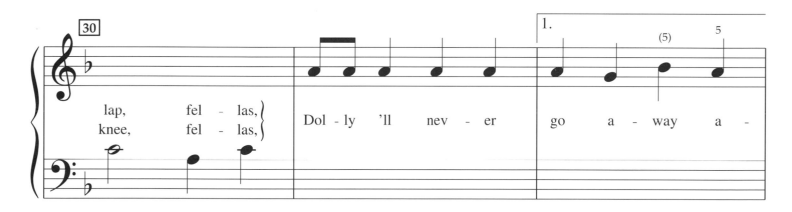

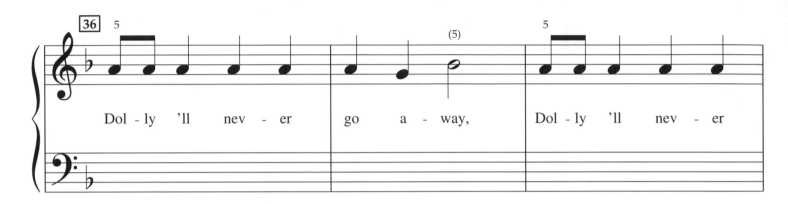

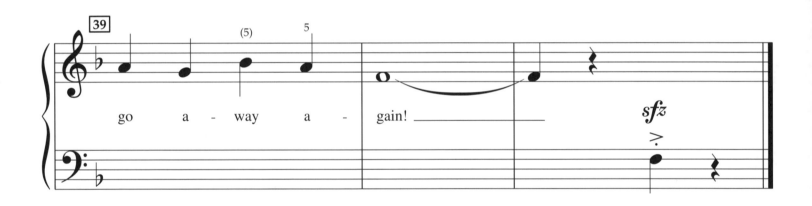

Memory
from CATS

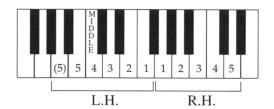

Music by Andrew Lloyd Webber
Text by Trevor Nunn after T.S. Eliot

Gently, in 1

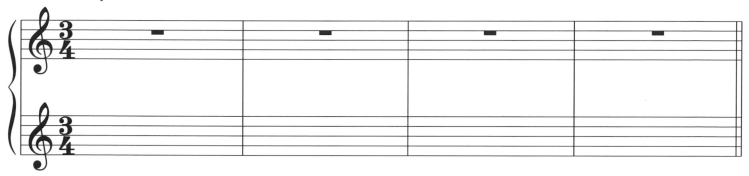

Mid - night. _____ Not a sound from the
Mem - ory _____ all a - lone in the

mp

Duet Part (Student plays one octave higher than written.)

Gently, in 1

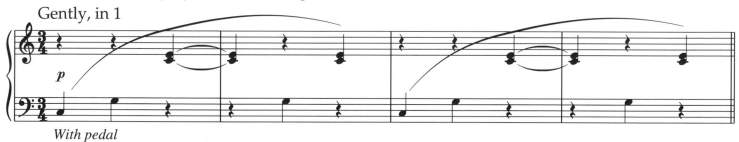

p

With pedal

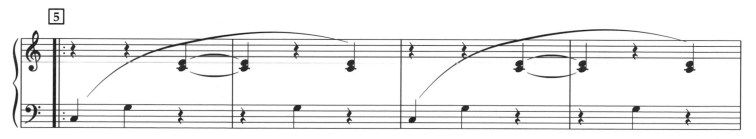

14

My Favorite Things
from THE SOUND OF MUSIC

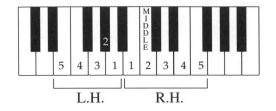

Lyrics by Oscar Hammerstein II
Music by Richard Rodgers

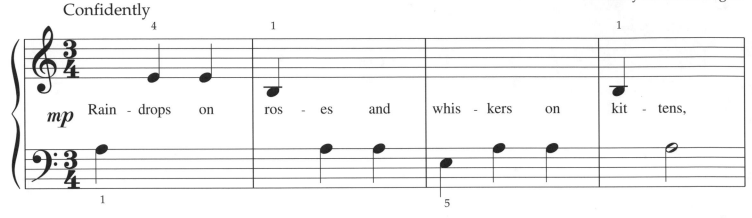

Rain - drops on ros - es and whis - kers on kit - tens,

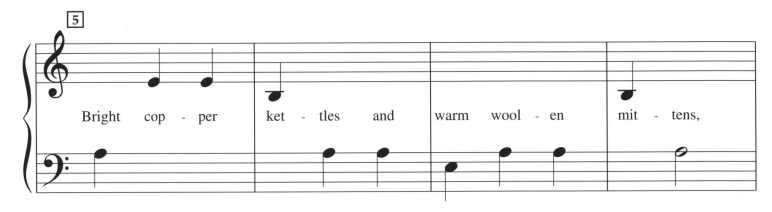

Bright cop - per ket - tles and warm wool - en mit - tens,

Duet Part (Student plays two octaves higher than written.)

Confidently

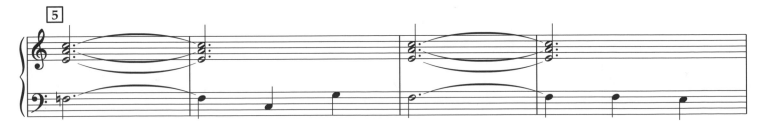

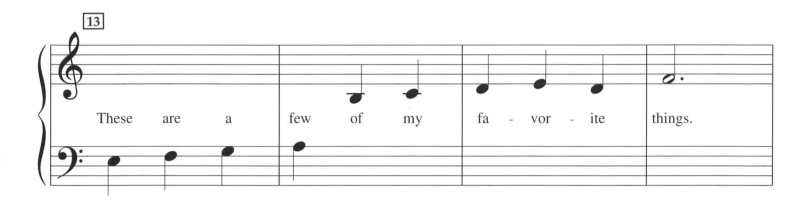

Brown pa - per pack - ag - es tied up with strings,
cresc.

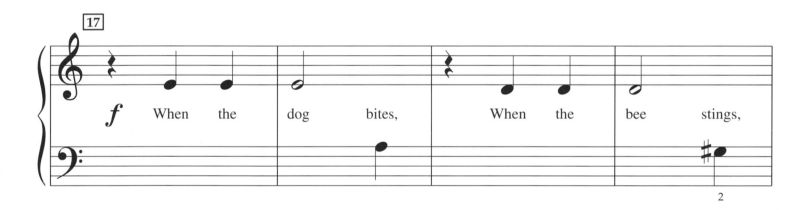

These are a few of my fa - vor - ite things.

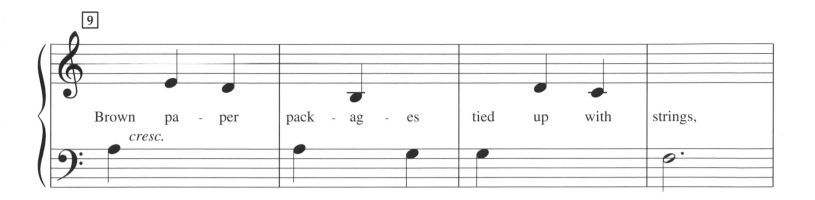

f When the dog bites, When the bee stings,

2

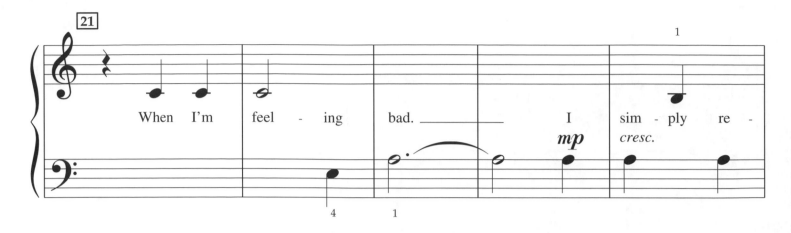

When I'm feel - ing bad. _____ I sim - ply re -

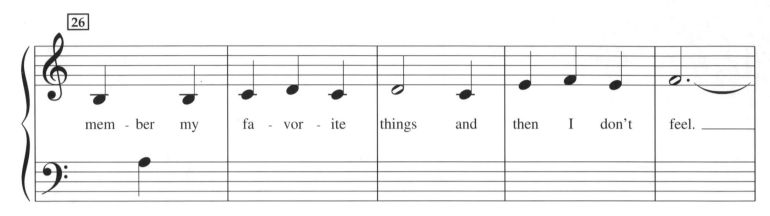

mem - ber my fa - vor - ite things and then I don't feel. _____

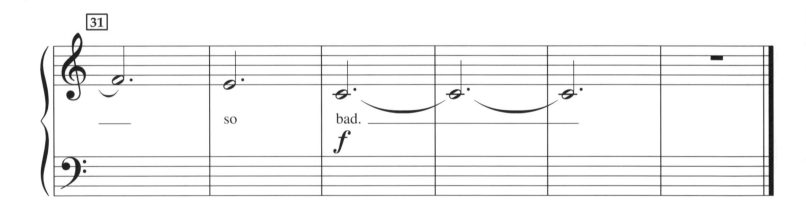

_____ so bad. _____

Oklahoma

from OKLAHOMA!

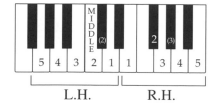

Lyrics by Oscar Hammerstein II
Music by Richard Rodgers

Brightly

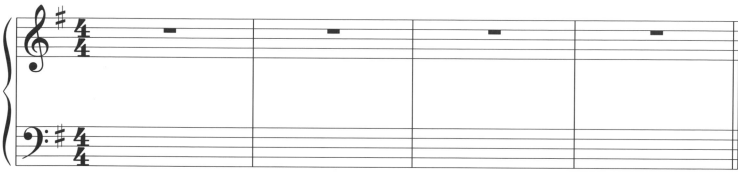

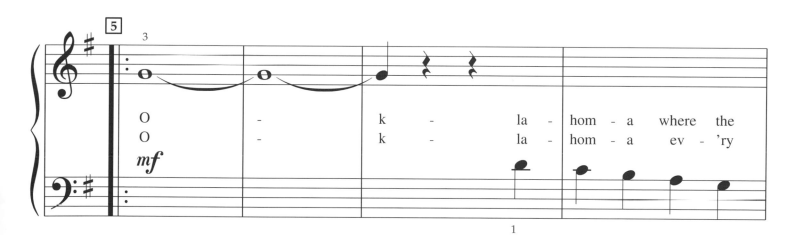

O - - k - la - hom - a where the
O - - k - la - hom - a ev - 'ry

mf

Duet Part (Student plays one octave higher than written.)

Brightly

mp   *cresc.*

mp

wind   comes   sweep - in'   down   the   plain,_____

night   my   hon - ey   lamb   and   I_____

(2)

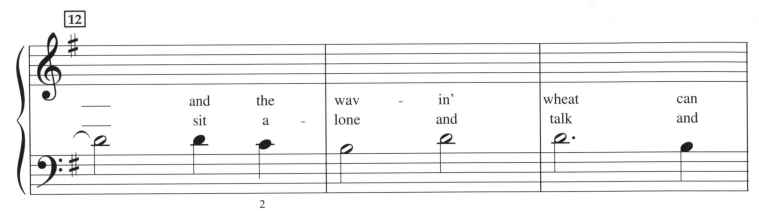

___   and   the   wav - in'   wheat   can

sit   a - lone   and   talk   and

2

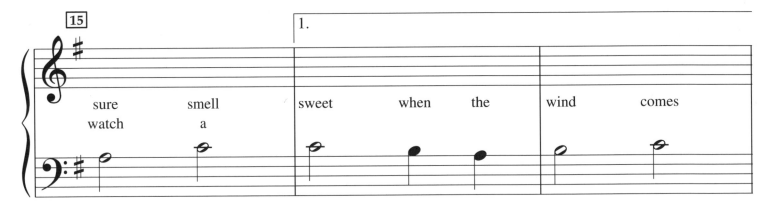

sure   smell   sweet   when   the   wind   comes

watch   a

1.

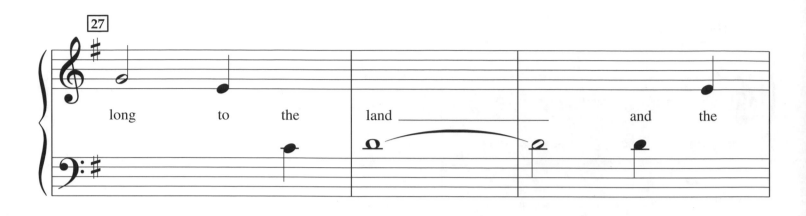

long to the land _____ and the

land we be - long to is grand! _____ And when we

mf

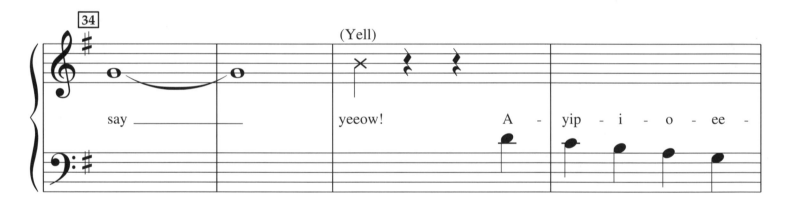

say _____ (Yell) yeeow! A - yip - i - o - ee -

mp

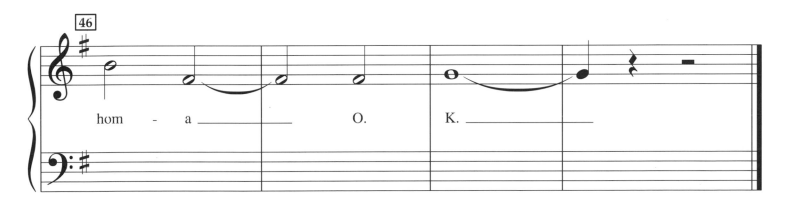

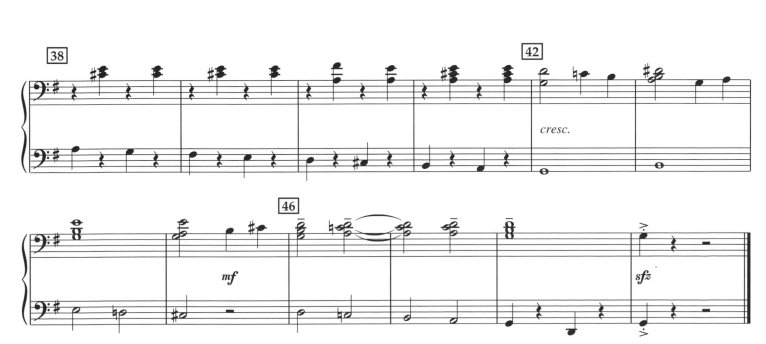

My Funny Valentine

from BABES IN ARMS

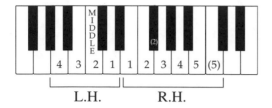

Words by Lorenz Hart
Music by Richard Rodgers

With expression

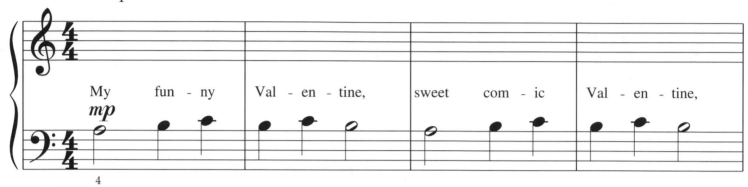

My fun-ny Val-en-tine, sweet com-ic Val-en-tine,

you make me smile with my heart.

Duet Part (Student plays one octave higher than written.)

With expression

With pedal

Your looks are laugh - a - ble, un - pho - to -

mp

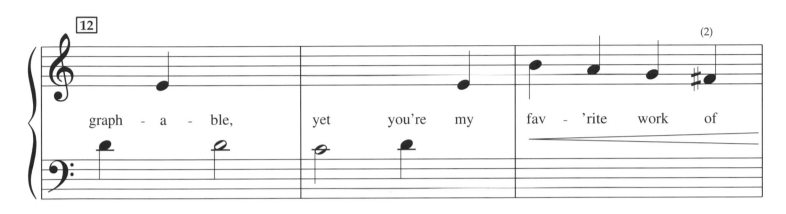

graph - a - ble, yet you're my fav - 'rite work of

(2)

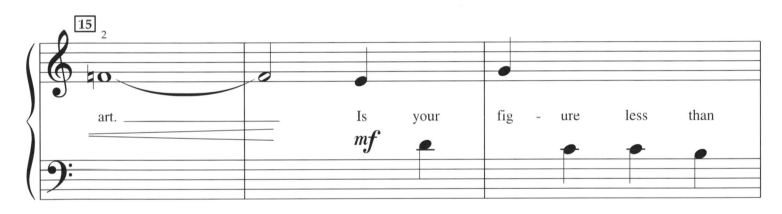

art. _____ Is your fig - ure less than

mf

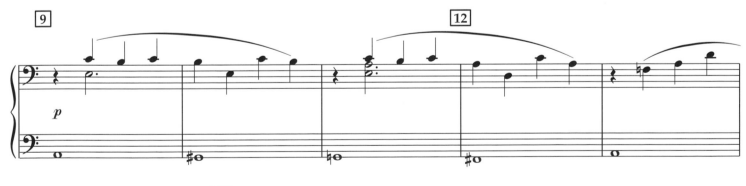

p

mp

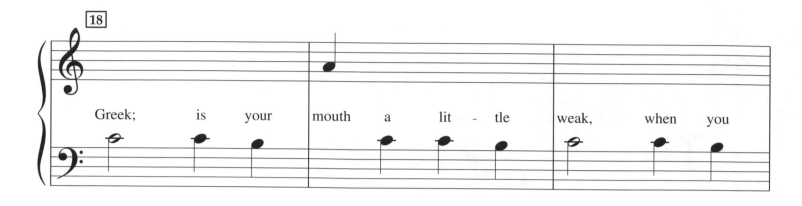

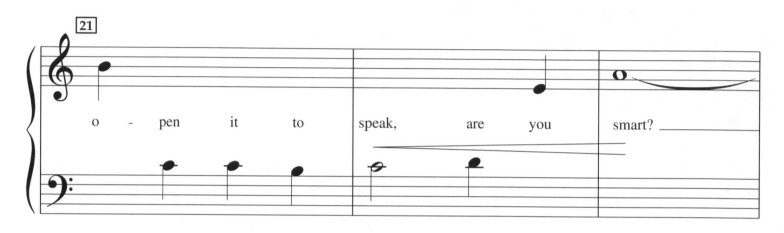

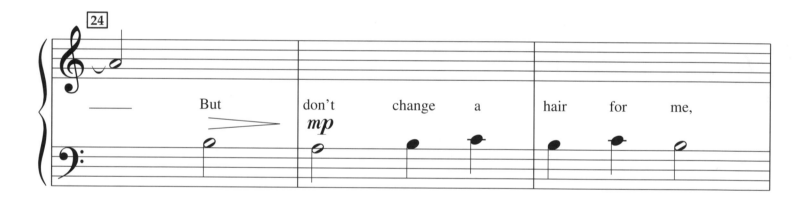

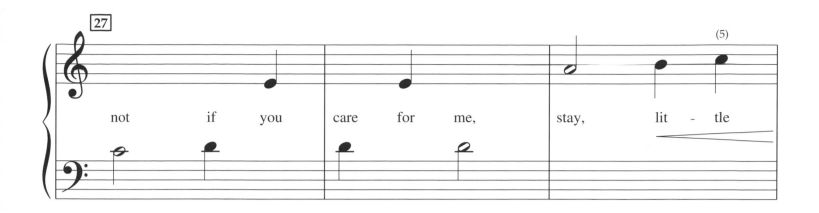

not   if   you   care   for   me,   stay,   lit - tle

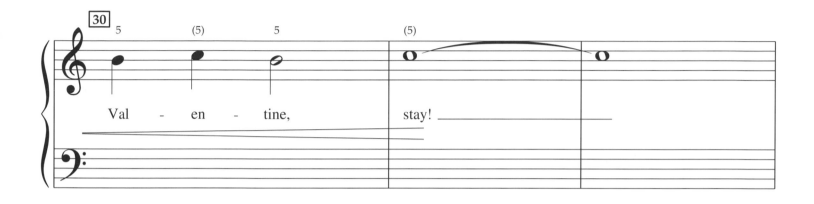

Val - en - tine,   stay! _____

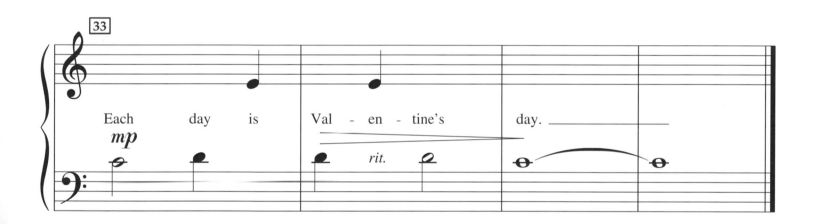

mp

Each   day   is   Val - en - tine's   day. _____

rit.

8vb

On My Own

from LES MISÉRABLES

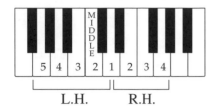

Music by Claude-Michel Schönberg
Lyrics by Alain Boublil, John Caird, Trevor Nunn,
Jean-Marc Natel and Herbert Kretzmer

Rather slowly, with feeling

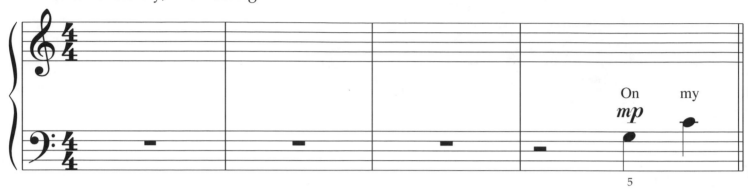

On my *mp*

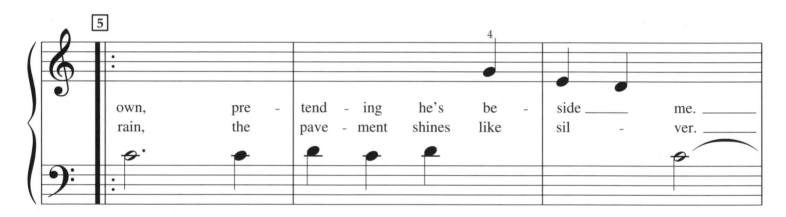

own, pre - tend - ing he's be - side _____ me. _____
rain, the pave - ment shines like sil - ver. _____

Duet Part (Student plays one octave higher than written.)

Rather slowly, with feeling

p

With pedal

p

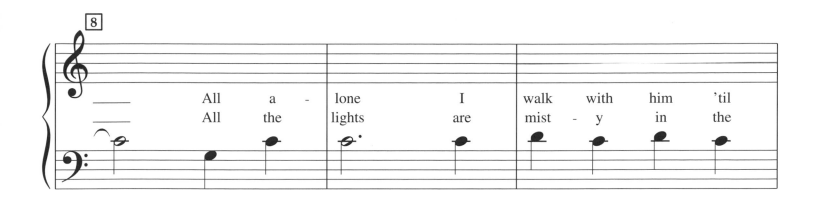

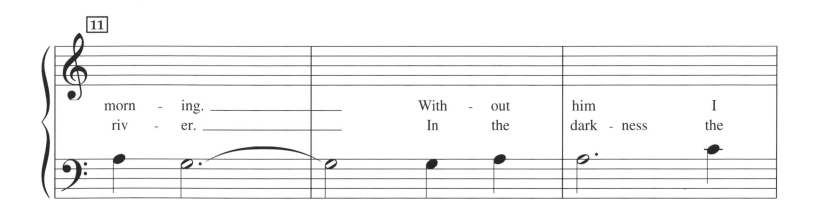

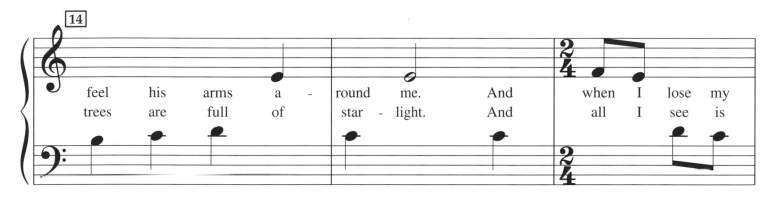

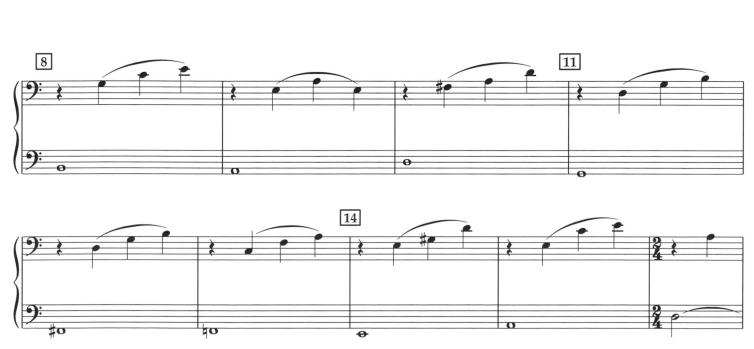

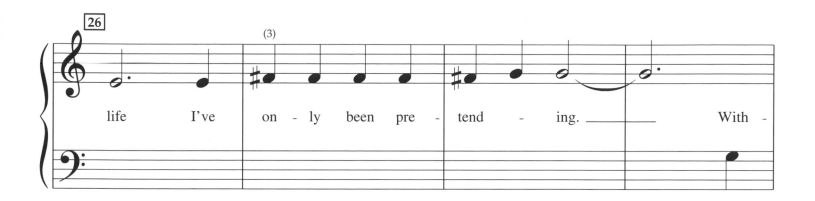

life I've on - ly been pre - tend - ing. _____ With -

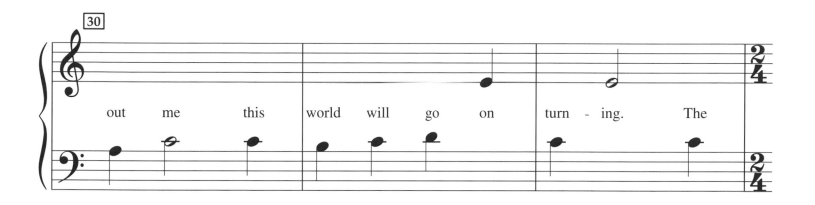

out me this world will go on turn - ing. The

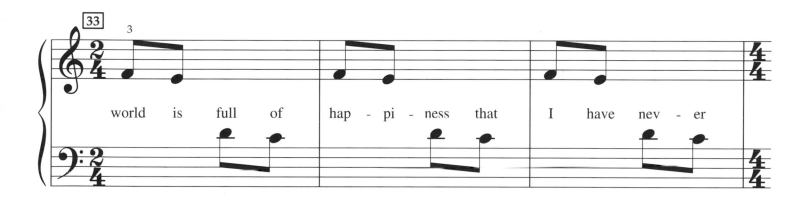

world is full of hap - pi - ness that I have nev - er

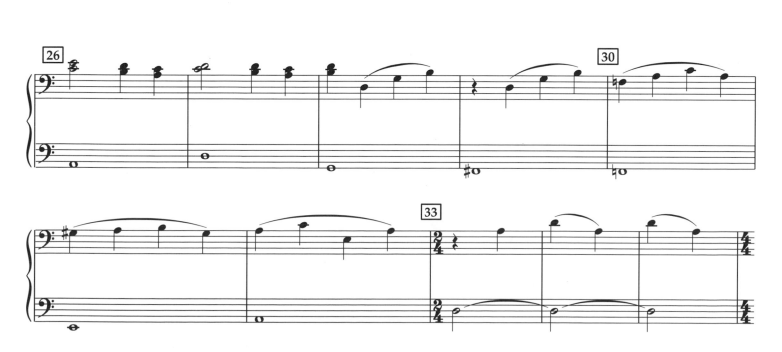

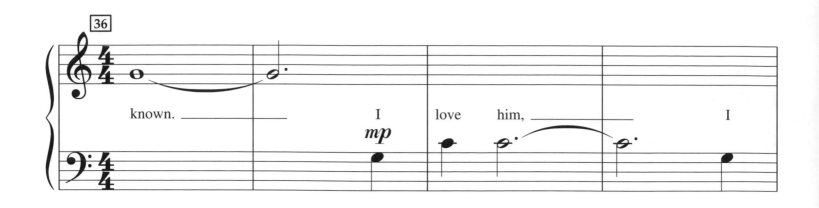

known. _____ I love him, _____ I

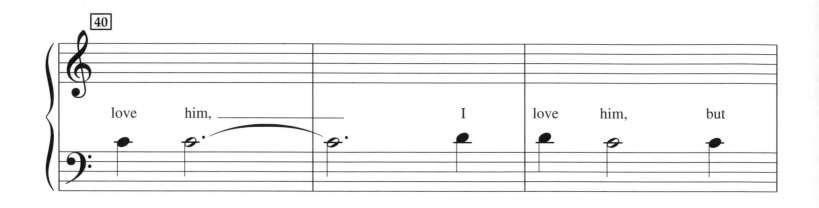

love him, _____ I love him, but

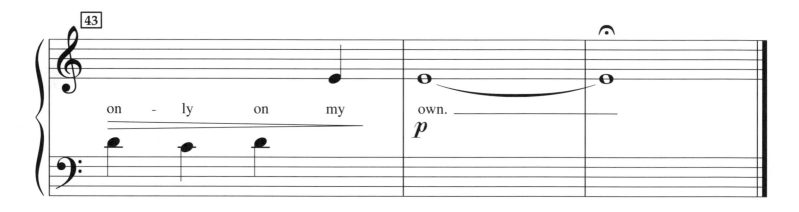

on - ly on my own. _____

People

from FUNNY GIRL

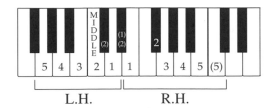

Words by Bob Merrill
Music by Jule Styne

Moderately, with expression

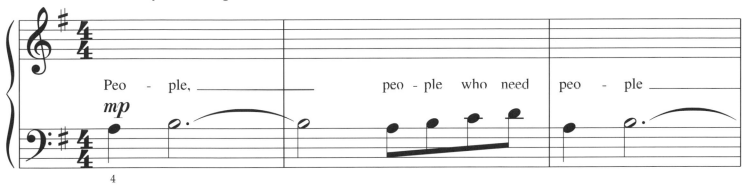

Peo - ple, _____ peo - ple who need peo - ple _____

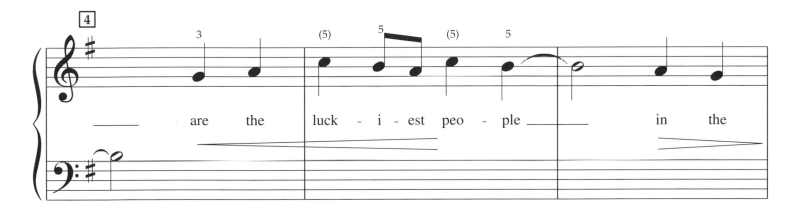

_____ are the luck - i - est peo - ple _____ in the

Duet Part (Student plays one octave higher than written.)

Moderately

With pedal

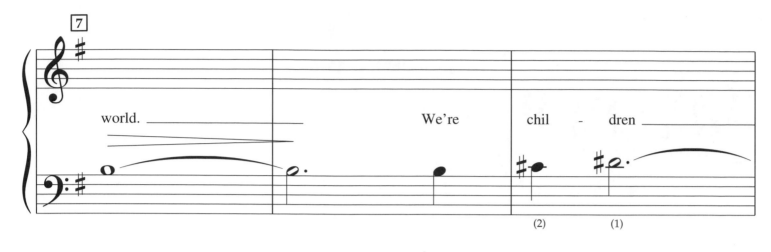

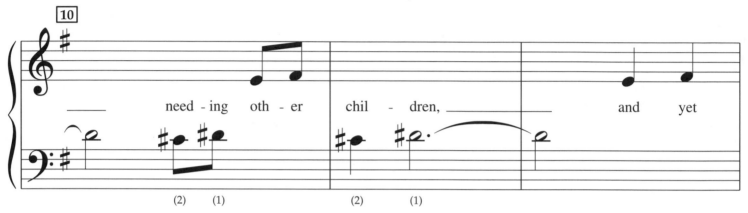

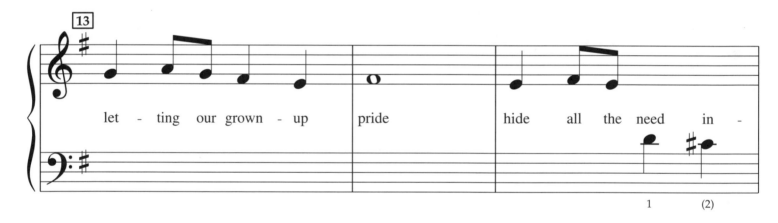

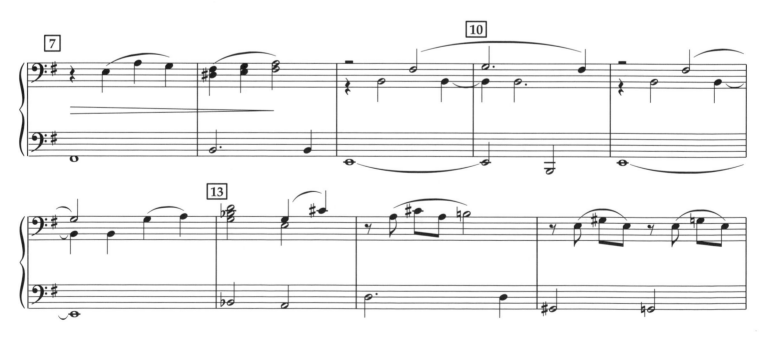

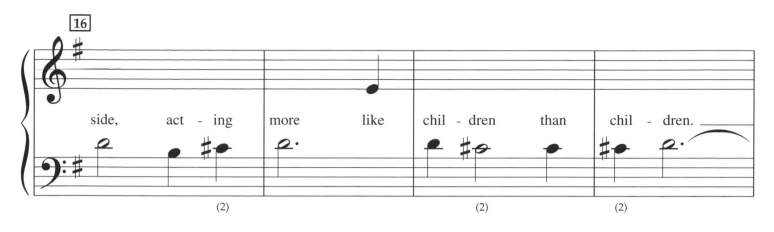

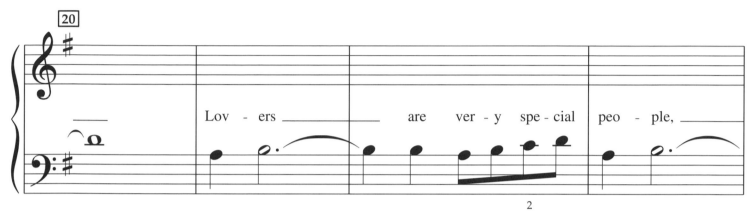

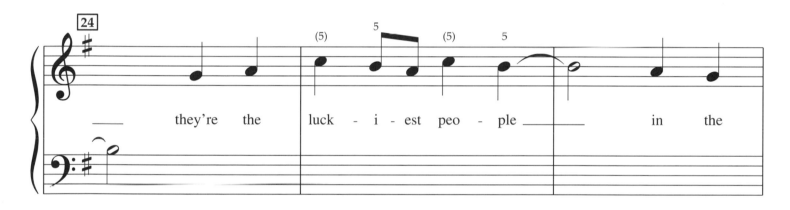

world. _____ With one per - son, _____

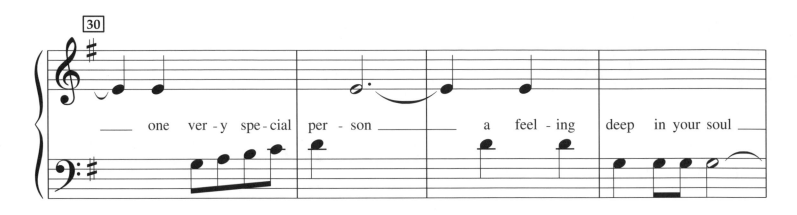

_____ one ver - y spe - cial per - son _____ a feel - ing deep in your soul _____

_____ says: you were half, now you're whole. _____ No more

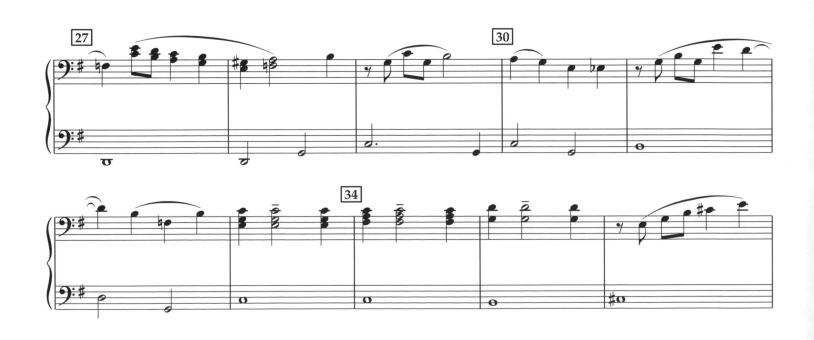

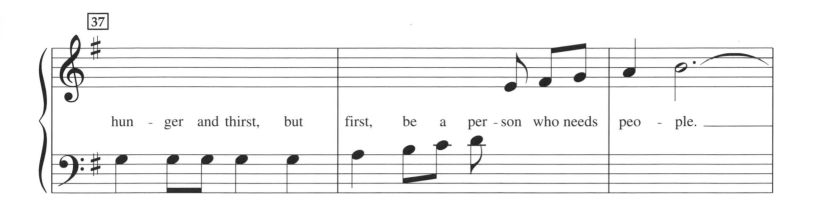

hun - ger and thirst, but first, be a per - son who needs peo - ple. _____

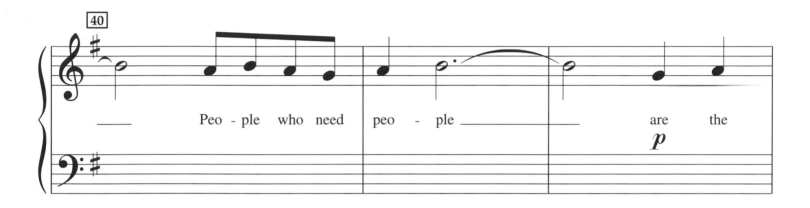

_____ Peo - ple who need peo - ple _____ are the

p

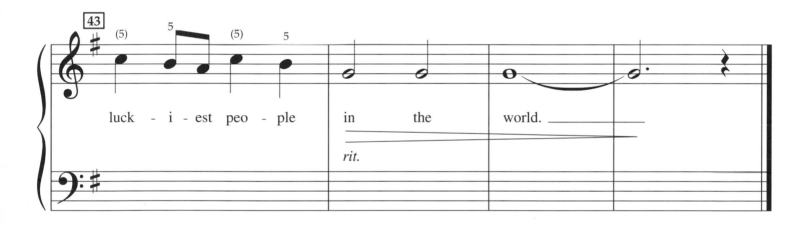

luck - i - est peo - ple in the world. _____

rit.

pp

rit.

What I Did for Love
from A CHORUS LINE

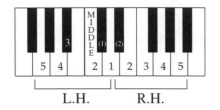

L.H.   R.H.

Music by Marvin Hamlisch
Lyrics by Edward Kleban

With expression

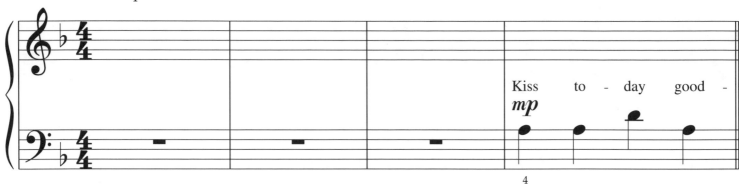

Kiss to-day good-

mp

4

bye, _____ the sweet-ness and the
dry, _____ the gift was ours to

Duet Part (Student plays one octave higher than written.)

With expression

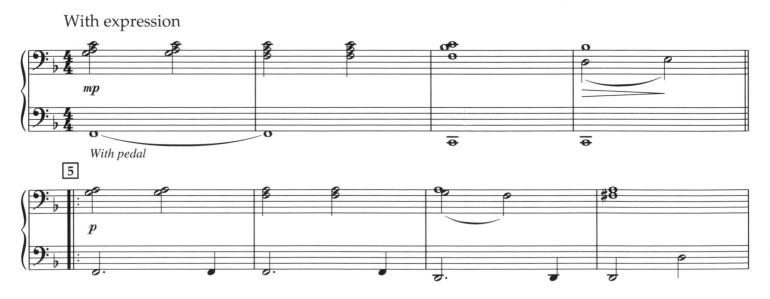

mp

With pedal

p

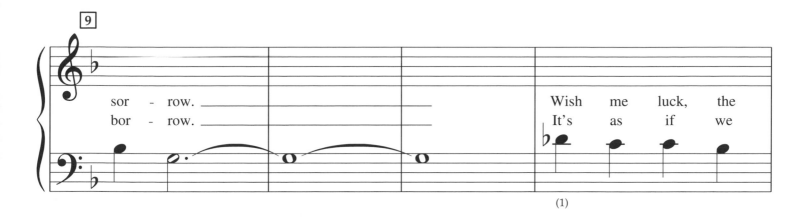

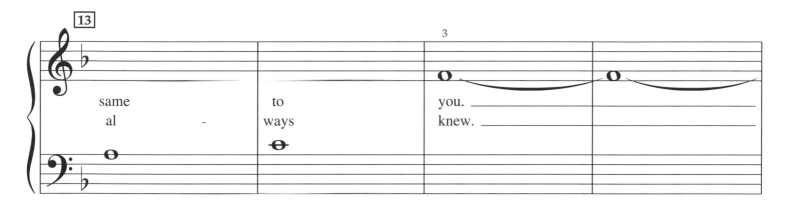

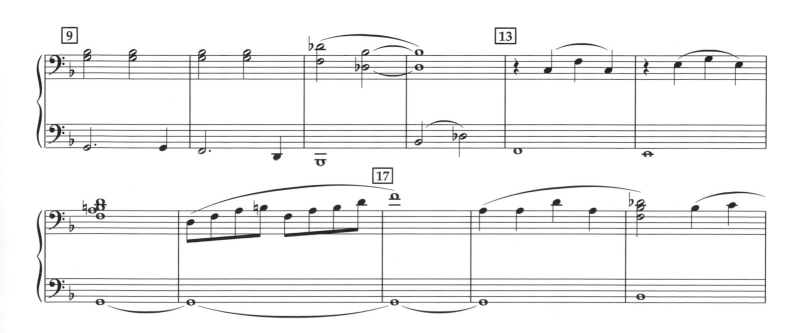

41

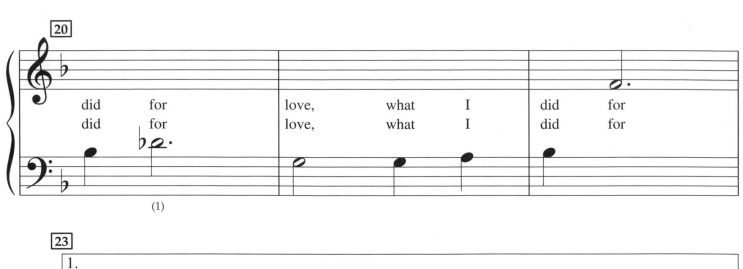

(1)

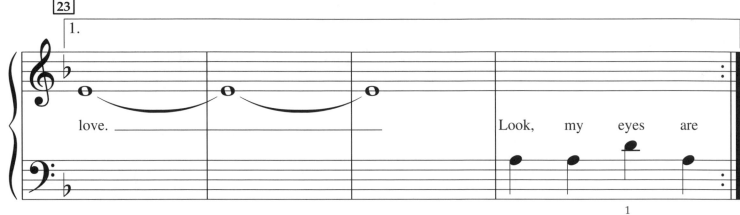

1

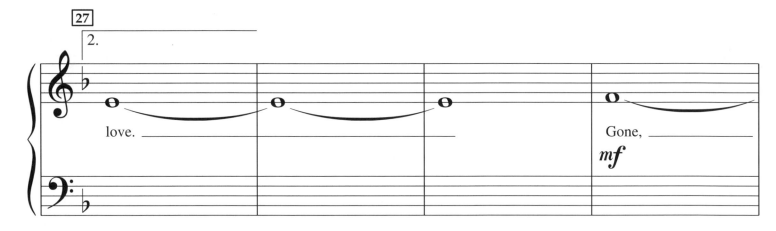

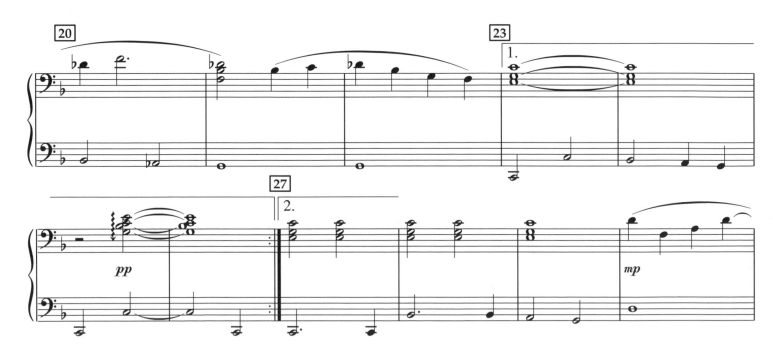

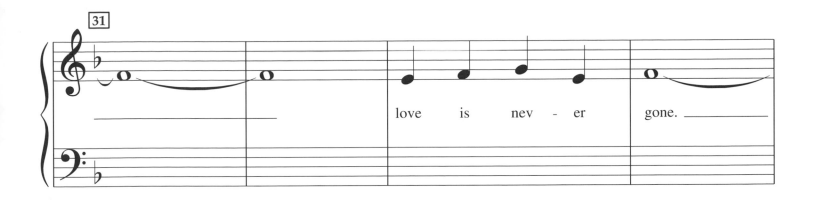

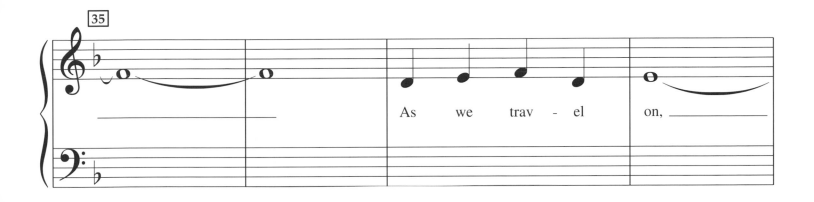

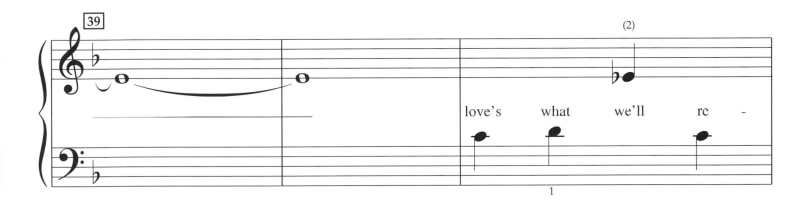

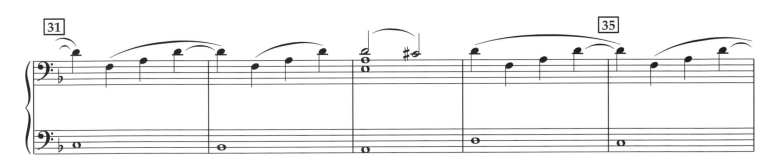

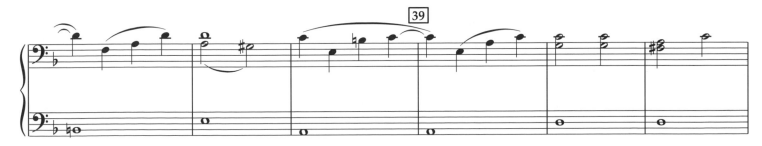

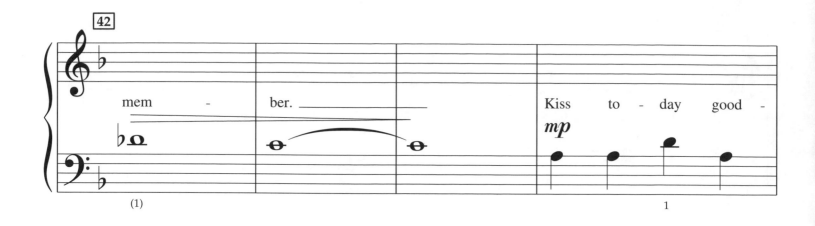

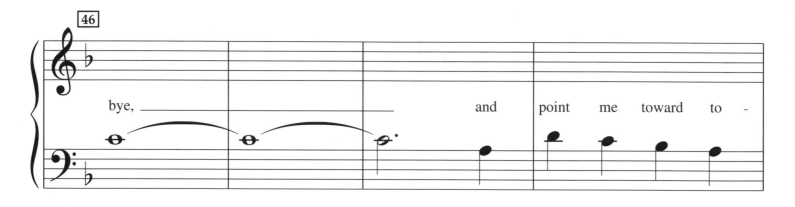

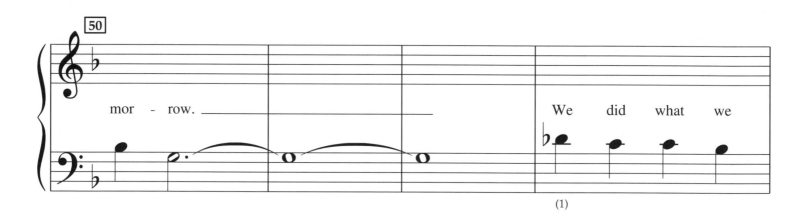

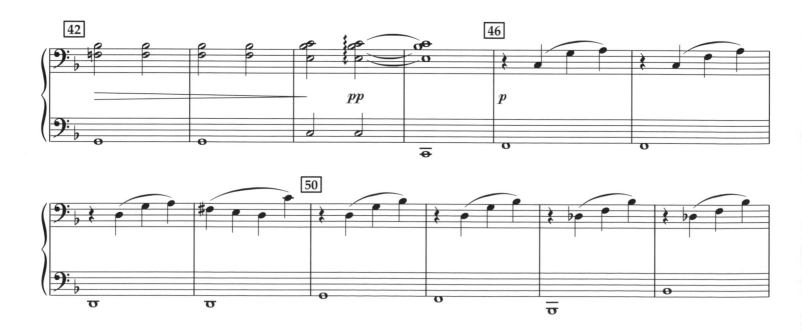

44

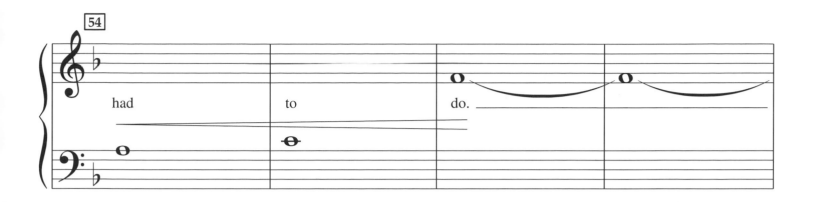

had   to   do. _____

Won't for - get, can't re-

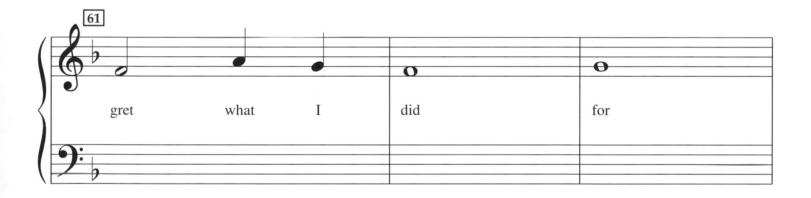

gret what I did   for

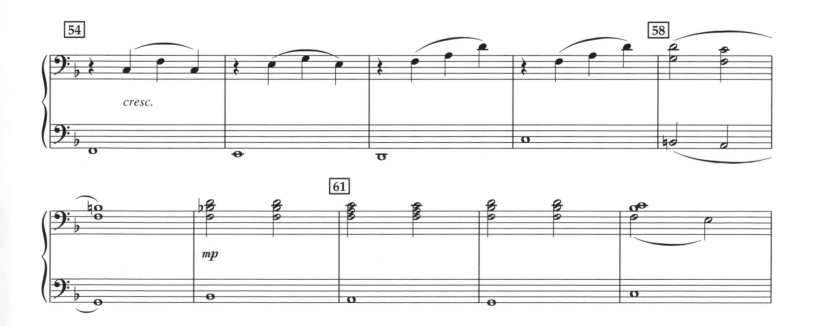

45

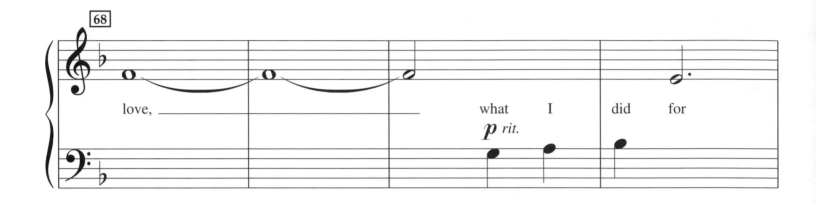

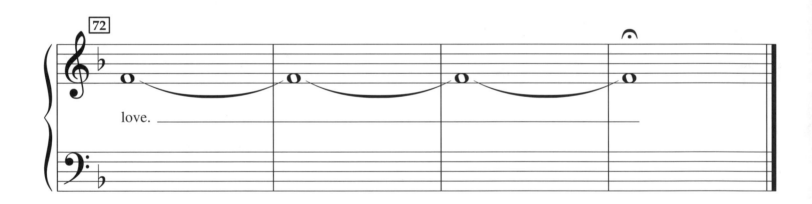

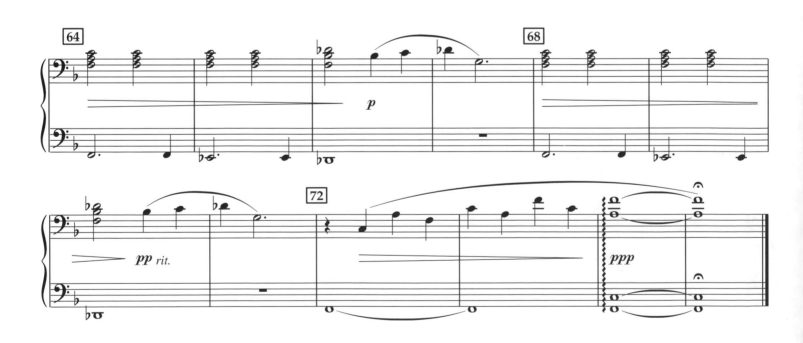

PLAYING PIANO HAS NEVER BEEN EASIER!

FIVE 5 FINGER PIANO

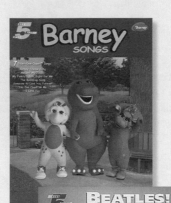

5-FINGER PIANO COLLECTIONS FROM HAL LEONARD

BARNEY SONGS

This five-finger piano book features seven Super-Dee-Duper™ songs! Includes: Barney Theme Song • I Love You • Me and My Teddy • My Family's Just Right for Me • The Raindrop Song • Someone to Love You Forever • You Can Count on Me.

_____00316065 ....$7.95

BEATLES! BEATLES!

8 classics, including: A Hard Day's Night • Hey Jude • Love Me Do • P.S. I Love You • Ticket to Ride • Twist and Shout • Yellow Submarine • Yesterday.

_____00292061 ....$7.95

CHURCH SONGS FOR KIDS

Features five-finger arrangements of 15 sacred favorites, including: Amazing Grace • The B-I-B-L-E • Down in My Heart • Fairest Lord Jesus • Hallelu, Hallelujah! • I'm in the Lord's Army • Jesus Loves Me • Kum Ba Yah • My God Is So Great, So Strong and So Mighty • Oh, How I Love Jesus • Praise Him, All Ye Little Children • Zacchaeus • and more.

_____00310613 ....$7.95

CLASSICAL FAVORITES

arr. Carol Klose

Includes 10 beloved classical pieces from Bach, Bizet, Haydn, Greig and other great composers: Bridal Chorus • Hallelujah! • He Shall Feed His Flock • Largo • Minuet in G • Morning • Rondeau • Surprise Symphony • To a Wild Rose • Toreador Song.

_____00310611 ....$7.95

CONTEMPORARY MOVIE HITS

7 favorite songs from hit films: Go the Distance (Hercules) • My Heart Will Go On (Titanic) • Remember Me This Way (Casper) • Someday (The Hunchback of Notre Dame) • When You Believe (The Prince of Egypt) • You'll Be in My Heart (Tarzan) • You've Got a Friend in Me (Toy Story and Toy Story II).

_____00310687 ....$7.95

DISNEY MOVIE FUN

8 classics, including: Beauty and the Beast • When You Wish Upon a Star • Whistle While You Work • and more.

_____00292067 ....$7.95

DISNEY TUNES

Includes: Can You Feel the Love Tonight? • Chim Chim Cher-ee • Go the Distance • It's a Small World • Supercalifragilisticexpialidocious • Under the Sea • You've Got a Friend in Me • Zero to Hero.

_____00310375 ....$7.95

EENSY WEENSY SPIDER & OTHER NURSERY RHYME FAVORITES

Includes 11 rhyming tunes kids love: Hickory Dickory Dock • Humpty Dumpty • Hush, Little Baby • Jack and Jill • Little Jack Horner • Mary Had a Little Lamb • Peter, Peter Pumpkin Eater • Pop Goes the Weasel • Tom, Tom, the Piper's Son • more.

_____00310465 ....$7.95

GOD BLESS AMERICA®

8 PATRIOTIC AND INSPIRATIONAL SONGS

Features 8 patriotic favorites anyone can play: America, the Beautiful • Battle Hymn of the Republic • God Bless America • My Country, 'Tis of Thee (America) • The Star Spangled Banner • This Is My Country • This Land Is Your Land • You're a Grand Old Flag.

_____00310828 ....$7.95

OUR FAVORITE FOLKSONGS

9 familiar favorites, including: The Blue Tail Fly (aka Jimmy Crack Corn) • Down in the Valley • Oh! Susanna • Yankee Doodle • and more.

_____00310068 ....$6.95

SUPER SILLY SONGS FOR FIVE FINGER PIANO

15 fun songs kids will love to play, including: Animal Fair • Be Kind to Your Web-Footed Friends • Do Your Ears Hang Low? • Little Bunny Foo Foo • The Man on the Flying Trapeze • A Peanut Sat on a Railroad Track • Who Threw the Overalls in Mrs. Murphy's Chowder • and more.

_____00310136 ....$7.95

TV TUNES

Easy arrangements of eight classic theme songs: The Ballad of Davy Crockett • The Brady Bunch • Fraggle Rock Theme • Mickey Mouse March • Mork and Mindy • The Muppet Show Theme • The Odd Couple • Rocky & Bullwinkle.

_____00310666 ....$7.95

0604

BIG FUN WITH BIG-NOTE PIANO BOOKS!
These songbooks feature exciting easy arrangements for beginning piano students.

And Now It's Time for Silly Songs with Larry

10 songs, including: The Dance of the Cucumber • Endangered Love • The Hairbrush Song • His Cheeseburger • Lost Puppies • Love My Lips • The Pirates Who Don't Do Anything • The Song of the Cebú • The Water Buffalo Songs • The Yodeling Veterinarian of the Alps.
00310836 ....$12.95

Best Songs Ever

73 favorites, featuring: Body and Soul • Born Free • Crazy • Edelweiss • Fly Me to the Moon • Georgia on My Mind • Imagine • The Lady Is a Tramp • Memory • A String of Pearls • Tears in Heaven • Unforgettable • You Are So Beautiful • more.
00310425 ....$19.95

Broadway Favorites

Bill Boyd

12 Broadway favorites for big-note piano, including: All I Ask of You • Edelweiss • Everything's Coming Up Roses • I Dreamed a Dream • Sunrise, Sunset • and more!
00290184 ....$8.95

Children's Favorites Movie Songs

16 favorites from films, including: The Bare Necessities • Beauty and the Beast • Can You Feel the Love Tonight • Do-Re-Mi • Feed the Birds • The Lonely Goatherd • My Funny Friend and Me • Raiders March • The Rainbow Connection • So Long, Farewell • Tomorrow • Yellow Submarine • You'll Be in My Heart (Pop Version) • Zip-A-Dee-Doo-Dah.
00310838 ....$10.95

Children's Favorites

14 songs children love, including: The Brady Bunch • Casper the Friendly Ghost • Going to the Zoo • The Grouch Song • Hakuna Matata • The Name Game • The Siamese Cat Song • Winnie the Pooh • more.
00310282 ....$7.95

A Christmas Collection

33 simplified favorites, including: The Christmas Song (Chestnuts Roasting) • Frosty the Snow Man • A Holly Jolly Christmas • I Saw Mommy Kissing Santa Claus • Mister Santa • The Most Wonderful Day of the Year • Nuttin' for Christmas • Silver Bells • and more.
00221818 ....$10.95

Classical Music's Greatest Hits

24 beloved classical pieces including: Air on the G String • Ave Maria • By the Beautiful Blue Danube • Canon in D • Eine Kleine Nachtmusik • Für Elise • Ode to Joy • Romeo and Juliet • Waltz of the Flowers • more.
00310475 ....$9.95

Country Favorites

28 songs, including: Achy Breaky Heart • Down at the Twist & Shout • God Bless the U.S.A. • Your Cheatin' Heart • and more.
00222554 ....$10.95

Disney's Princess Collection

26 songs of love and hope, including: Belle • Can You Feel the Love Tonight • Colors of the Wind • Home • Kiss the Girl • Love • Part of Your World • Reflection • Some Day My Prince Will Come • Something There • A Whole New World • and more.
00316084 ....$14.95

Great Jazz Standards

arranged by Bill Boyd

20 songs, including: April in Paris • Don't Get Around Much Anymore • How High the Moon • It Don't Mean a Thing (If It Ain't Got That Swing) • When I Fall in Love • and more.
00222575 ....$12.95

God Bless America

15 patriotic songs, including Irving Berlin's classic title song and: America, the Beautiful • Battle Hymn of the Republic • A Mighty Fortress Is Our God • My Country, 'Tis of Thee (America) • O God, Our Help in Ages Past • The Star Spangled Banner • Stars and Stripes Forever • This Is My Country • This Land Is Your Land • We Shall Overcome • and more.
00310827 ....$9.95

Hymn Favorites

Includes 20 favorite hymns: Abide with Me • Blest Be the Tie That Binds • Jesus Loves Me • Nearer My God to Thee • Rock of Ages • What a Friend We Have in Jesus • and more.
00221802 ....$6.95

Les Misérables

14 songs, including: At the End of the Day • Bring Him Home • Castle On a Cloud • Do You Hear the People Sing • I Dreamed a Dream • In My Life • On My Own • and more.
00221812 ....$14.95

TV Hits

Over 20 theme songs that everyone knows, including: Brady Bunch • Cheers • (Meet) The Flintstones • Home Improvement • The Jetsons • Northern Exposure • Mr. Ed • The Munsters Theme • Won't You Be My Neighbor • and more fun favorites!
00221805 ....$9.95

Prices, contents, and availability subject to change without notice. Disney artwork © Disney Enterprises, Inc.

FOR MORE INFORMATION, SEE YOUR LOCAL MUSIC DEALER,
OR WRITE TO:

HAL•LEONARD®
CORPORATION
7777 W. BLUEMOUND RD. P.O. BOX 13819 MILWAUKEE, WI 53213

www.halleonard.com

0903